On The Truth Of Decorative Art......

Lionel de Fonseka

ON THE TRUTH

OF

DECORATIVE ART

On the Truth
of
Decorative Art

A Dialogue between an
Oriental and an Occidental

By
Lionel de Fonseka

New Popular Issue

New York:
Henry Holt & Co.
1913

Dedicated
In respect and affection
to
Simon   Richard   de   Fonseka
Warnesuriya   Wijetunge   Samaranayake,
Mudaliyar   of   the   Gate,
and
Mudaliyar   of   Salpiti   Korle,   Ceylon.

PREFATORY NOTE.

THIS dialogue is written primarily for the people of Ceylon. Sinhalese art has hitherto been strictly decorative; and as a Sinhalese I view with regret the modern tendency in Ceylon, under Western influences, to abandon our traditions in art and in life. It seems to me that Eastern peoples need to realize at the least that *art*, *education*, *civilization*, admit of a plural; also that what is fortuitously predominant is not necessarily intrinsically excellent. It is regrettable that the rise of Western commerce should involve the decline of Eastern art; but though regrettable, it is not inevitable.

I would remind the Sinhalese people of the best traditions of our art by calling to mind a work of our King, *Detu Tissa*, an artist of the 4th century, who, in the words of the *Mahawansa*, "was a skilful carver, who executed many arduous undertakings in painting, and taught it to his subjects. *He modelled a statue of Buddha so exquisitely that he seemed to have been inspired; and for it he made an altar, and gilt an edifice inlaid with ivory.*"

ON THE TRUTH

OF

DECORATIVE ART

A DIALOGUE
BETWEEN AN ORIENTAL AND AN OCCIDENTAL

I.

ON DECORATING LIFE.

I.

ON DECORATING LIFE.

"HAVE you seen this article in the *Journal of Side Issues*? Here is another artist complaining that the painter's opportunities are limited now-a-days because life is not sufficiently picturesque."

" Well, how does he propose to make life picturesque ? "

" He suggests among other things that costume-balls should be made more fashionable than they are, so that ordinary life too might have, as he says, something of the quality of a masquerade. He believes that the present popularity of pageants is a hopeful sign in that they bring home to people the colourlessness of modern life by contrast."

" Does he ? I should say that the modern taste for pageants is most ominous. You have been having so many pageants lately, and charging for admission to them at so much per head, that you think the only proper place for a pageant is an enclosed area. You seem to think that the first essential of a pageant is a paling. Consequently you will never make a pageant of life— or ever have a pageant in real life."

" We had one last year—the pageant of the Coronation. I suppose you were in London at the time. What did you think of the Coronation and the English expression of festivity ? "

" I really don't know what to think of it. It was said by some at the time that the Coronation was a failure. I wonder if it was. I am inclined to think rather that the English, and Western peoples generally, have lost the faculty of expression. Of course, it may be that the whole ceremony and pomp of the Coronation had no significance for the people—that it was a masquerade enacted by a few chosen actors, leaving—to borrow a phrase from your politicians—the mass of the people untouched. But I am unwilling to believe it. Where there is no sentiment of course one could not expect an expression. But from my own observations I am led to believe that the necessary sentiment did exist among the people—at least there was a disposition to encourage it—a mood like that of a man about to fall in love, who gives free rein to his imagination. But the English people failed on that occasion to give expression not only to the sentiment but even to its begetting mood. Western peoples have been hankering after needless expression so long that when there is an opportunity and a call for exuberant expression, they cannot rise to it. They have no artistic sense."

" That is a very comprehensive, and, if I may say so, a slightly original remark. Anyhow what do you mean by an artistic sense ? "

" In this case I suppose I mean a sense of the fitness of things. Did you notice the Coronation "decorations" in Whitehall ? I believe those particular decorations were meant to give expression to the Imperial sentiment. It may be that the expression produced was a fitting one. If that was so, I should have to credit the artist responsible for its production with a spirit of sad irony."

" How do you mean ? "

" Well, did it not strike you as being rather a petrified expression ?— ' Triumphal arches' in stucco, and those columns erected with such regularity and precision. Did not the whole thing appear machine-made ? But, as I said,

I am unwilling to judge the sentiment by the expression. I prefer to think that Western peoples do not understand expression."

" You amaze me."

" In the East now, we use a profusion of palm-leaves and greenery on festive occasions, a usage that obtained also in early Christendom. You will remember the observance of Palm Sunday still preserved in the Catholic Church. ' But,' you will object, ' We have no palm-leaves in England.' Maybe, but there are flowers in the fields. Why so much tinsel and tissue-paper? However, this is only one instance, and that a disputable one, of the current Western misunderstanding of expression. My remark holds good. Western peoples do not understand expression."

" In what way ? "

" In this way perhaps. In the West, expression is held to be the function of art. In the East we believe that the end of art is decoration. The difference between these two theories of art is at once the symbol and the reason of the difference between East and West. It affects the whole ordering of the lives of the East and of the West."

" I am afraid I must insist on some further explanation."

" I will explain as well as I can. In the first place, you Westerns have no artistic sense. I mean by this a sense of the fitness of things, though it may seem idle to talk of an 'artistic sense' when the matter at issue is the difference between two theories of art. But, you see, as an Eastern, I include life as coming within the scope of the artistic sense,—and in precisely such a sense, a sense of artistic living, you appear to be lacking. Hence the artistic errors of the Coronation—errors which we could never have committed, since our theory of art would have saved us from them. You have been led into these errors through your wrong notion of expression. You are too self-conscious about art and about expression. You are always trying to express yourselves. We never do—neither in art nor in life. You aim at expression and fail. We aim at repression and succeed,—and incidentally achieve expression as well. That your expressions fail, however, is not in itself a proof that you are not sound at heart. The festive expression you evoked for the Coronation was a failure. But do not be despondent on that account about the Monarchy or the Empire. Expression is apt to lie."

" I am a loyal subject of His Majesty, and following the Birmingham mode, my thought is tinged with the rosy hue of Imperialism. For the sake of my peace of mind you will perhaps cite some instances of lying expression."

" The hue of Imperialism is not rosy but scarlet. That cast of thought alone is not pale but clamorously ruddy ; and wisely do you paint the Empire red on your maps, there for once contriving a truthful expression. But we are concerned rather with lying expression. Just now, decorative dancing, as you know, is much in vogue in Europe. It is a good sign. It has not been so always. You will remember Isidora Duncan and Maud Allan, and the Russian Dancers at Covent Garden. Well, in the East decorative dancing has always been in favour, but not ball-room dancing. Ball-room dancing, by the way, when it is not a giddy gallop is an inane shuffle. It is either too much or too little civilized. I was present at some London balls recently. In half the dances the dancers seemed intensely bacchic, and in the other half they seemed intensely bored—which convinced me that ball-room dancing is

not a form of art. It certainly is not
beautiful. Eastern ladies have never
countenanced balls, though they admire
decorative dances by professional
dancers—the dances of geishas and
nautch-girls for instance. It was so with
Romans of the austere, aristocratic
temper. They would not dance themselves, but gladly looked on the dancing
of others. 'No one dances except when
not sober,' said Cicero. Ball-room
dancing in Europe is often only a convention. As an expression it may be
too expressive. It is too near akin to
the actor's art. No spiritual aristocrat
will prostitute his expressions to the
emotions of another. The most gentle
aristocrats will not give free expression
to their own emotions. That Eastern
ladies should have rejected so immediate
a form of expression as personal dancing
is the proof of an exquisitely eclectic
taste. So that when you hear people
objecting to the 'promiscuous dancing

9

of the ball-room,' you need not infer that they are prudes. It is possible that you have been misreading your history oftener than you think. Cromwell and his Roundheads were in truth more courtly—regal after the Aurelian fashion—than Charles and his courtly Cavaliers. The Puritans were men of a rare preciosity. What was mistaken for Philistinism was really their fastidiousness—present day Quakers still retain a degree of their ancestors' quaintness. The Commonwealth Iconoclasts were æsthetes who had the courage of their æsthetic theory and happened to be energetic. They were the Futurists of the past. The Futurists of the present day are, as you know, admitted on all hands to be Decadents in the last stage of decay. Expressions, you see, are often treacherous and misleading. I can cite a more recent and more particular instance of ambiguous expression. Judged by his appearance and his attire, Baudelaire, that master of Decadence, might have been taken for a Genevan cleric. Which expression should you trust ?—for a waist-coat is an expression no less than a prose-poem, provided of course that the waist-coat is worn for its own sake without any idea of creating an impression. If Truth is Beauty, the fact that expression is apt to lie is an argument for pure decoration as an artistic end. At any rate, conscious expression is, I fear, an artistic error."

" But surely artistic achievement lies simply in the conscious expression of personal emotion."

"Ah yes, one hears that said very often. Did not Oscar Wilde say, ' Now-adays a broken heart runs into many editions ' ? But at other times Wilde himself prattled much about intensity of feeling. Some people would break their hearts deliberately in order that the editions might have a sale. Who was the French writer who said that the world was made in order that a beautiful book might be written ? We believe that the world was made to live and die in— especially to die in. No ; one should aim not at intensity but at rarity of feeling. Emotion, you say, is necessary to artistic achievement. What is more desirable is a mood. A mood is a rarified emotion. A mood precludes conscious expression, yet it leaves its reflection on the artistic product, as the mood of a parent when begetting is said to shed a shadow or a radiance on the life of the offspring. It is only when thus rarified that an emotion can, in any true sense, ' be translated into a medium.' But more often people pour their feelings chaotically into receptacles. The melting hearts run into the many editions. In the Potter's Shop of art the vessel takes its shape from its contents. Hence it is that so many of your would-be artistic vessels, far from being vessels of election, are

absolutely formless. The Greeks knew
the value of moods. The freizes and
pediments of their temples, and their
vases were reflections of moods. The
Grecian Urn commemorated by Keats
was a mood translated into a medium.
Tennyson's *In Memoriam* was an
emotion spilt into an elegy. Which is
the more vital art—the decoration of the
vase which was meant to express nothing
and symbolizes much, or the elegy which
was meant to express feeling, but
succeeds only in expressing failure?"

" But surely, if you bar feeling, you
must supply some other motive for
artistic creation. One can do nothing,
at least one can do nothing well, without
a motive."

" Quite true. I do not say that we
bar all feeling in Eastern art. We forbid
the conscious expression of personal
feeling. As for motives, there are other
motives than the selfish, just as there

are many feelings, many moods other
than the personal."

"I dare say. But of what value for
art are such motives and such feelings?
An art which lacks the personal motive
must be frigid, and an art unprompted
by personal feeling must be conventional.
Art should above all things be human—
arising from human needs and quickening
human sympathies. You remember
Miranda's words, 'I have suffered with
those I have seen suffer.' And do we
too not suffer with Miranda on the
Island, and share Lear's anguish on
the heath,—and weep with Niobe over
her stricken children? Are we not
maddened with something of Medea's
jealousy and despair when she is moved
to poision her babes, and share
Laocoon's helpless terror when he would
save his sons from the dread monsters?
Do we not weep with Dido when she
sees Æneas depart from Tyre?"

"And with George Sand when she sees de Musset leave Venice for Switzerland? You might weep once, but George Sand repeated her emotions, and I take it you would not care to weep anew over each repetition. All George Sand's and most modern novels might well bear the title *Elle et Lui*. If you thus reiterate the emotion, why not re-echo the title? You might perhaps have *Lui et Elle* for a variation. You say that an art unprompted by personal feeling must be conventional, hinting that personal feeling must save, art from convention. But it is abundantly clear that that form of Western art which is classified in your literary reviews under the head of 'Recent Fiction' suffers seriously from the convention of a particular personal feeling. I cannot understand the term 'Recent Fiction' either, since the fiction is as ancient as the Garden of Eden. And what is a fiction which isn't fresh? It is a convention."

" If conventions then confessedly are fossilized lies, does not Eastern art stand condemned, being, as it is, almost entirely an art of conventions? You criticize Western art as based on expression, which, you say, is apt to lie. How about Eastern art which apparently lives on falsehood? Or is Truth not Beauty? "

" Yes, conventions are confessedly fossilized lies—and the fact of being conventional, which you hurl at Eastern art as a reproach, we accept merely as a qualification. But consider—a confessed lie is no longer a lie, and a lie whose falsehood was professed before it was ever uttered was never a lie at all. In the sphere of ethics such lies are called parables; in literature they are allegories; in art they are symbols. In so far as it speaks in symbols then, Eastern art is conventional, as every art which speaks in symbols must be.

Your art is conventional because it speaks in parables. Your symbols are cautionary signs, and your allegories cautionary tales. So that your art is conventional not by virtue of its artistic essence, but by reason of the ethical element which dominates your art. It is of the nature of Eastern art to be conventional. The conventionalism of Western art is a disease."

" Surely now you are quibbling, or —to borrow a euphemism from the Greeks—you are saying nothing. How could the same thing be health in one art and disease in another art? If conventions are a disease in Western art—a contention which I do not admit, since I deny that Western art is conventional—they must be so in Eastern art as well. Is not all art one? So that the nature or constitution of Eastern art could not be different from the nature or constitution of Western art, and what is health or disease in the one must be health or disease in the other."

" Conventions in Eastern art are a property. In Western art they are an affection. Consider art as an organism. A property of an organism comes of its nature or constitution, when the members of the organism are in harmony with each other,—when, in other words, the organism is in a state of health. An affection, on the other hand, arises when the members are at discord. In Plato's words, a harmony perishes when the elements composing it are not at the right tension. Now in Western art, the *ethical* element is inharmoniously predominant. Your art is too exclusively ethical—*ethical* in the derivative sense of having a moral bias, and also in the immediate sense of being too much concerned with character—with *Ethos*, in the Aristotelian sense of the word. The conventions of Eastern art belong to form, where they are natural. The conventions of Western art belong to matter, and are an affection. And that is why I say that Eastern art is conventional by virtue of its artistic essence, which amounts to saying that formal conventions are a necessary condition of art. Convention belongs to form,—it is the virtue of form. Material conventions on the other hand are repugnant to art. They arise when the organism of art is out of harmony through the undue predominance of some element. So you will understand my remark that the conventionalism of Western art is a disease, vitiating your art for this further reason also, that your material conventions are essentially false conventions."

"Don't you think you are disposed to be a trifle arrogant, in thus demanding the excellence of Eastern, and derogating without warrant the excellence of Western art? Did we not agree in this at any rate, that all conventions are lies?"

"Conventions we agreed to regard as confessed lies. The symbols of Eastern art, conventions of form, are accepted by us as lies. That is to say, we realize that they symbolize, that they stand for something, very often for an unknown quantity. In themselves, we know that they are nothing, or if you prefer it, are not real. And so these symbols contain an essence of truth. It is different with your conventions of matter. They are lies, but they are unconfessed lies, and so they hold an essence of falsehood. In fact lies of matter, by their very nature, cannot be confessed, because they are literally *substantial* lies, and their essence is their falsehood. You cannot deny the reality of your conventions without denying the truth of your art. And so it is that material conventions are disease in art. An art that deals in material conventions truly lives on falsehood. Yours is an art of self-conscious expression, and such expression inevitably lies. The exaggeration of the ethical element in your art is the direct outcome of self-conscious expression."

"Would you think me very troublesome if I asked you to instance some particular material conventions?"

"Well, there is the convention of Love—the theme of all your novelists and dramatists—a material convention which colours all your art and particularly pervades your music. Wagner's is of course erotic music in its most accentuated form, but all your music is similarly tinged. Instead of being as it was with the Greeks, and is with Orientals, the most 'imitative' of the arts, comprehending life in all its variety, symbolizing the ideal harmony of life, and initiating men into the art of living, it is with you merely an initiation into the art of Love."

"Surely you are unjust. What of the music of the Salvation Army?"

"That is the martial music of militant Christianity. Truly religious music is of course an exception, and the reason of it is that it is decorative art. Music is often instanced as the type of all the arts, as art at its highest expression, in the algebraical sense, and with music for the type, one could see the truth of decorative as against expressive art. You often make it the peculiar excellence of your music that it is 'pure,' meaning that it is purely expressive, that it does not contain moral lessons as your drama is apt to do, that it does not like your novels draw attention to crying social evils, and that unlike architecture, it is entirely divorced from utility. Here apparently is an art whose end is purely æsthetic pleasure. But did not that truly Oriental philosopher, Plato, draw attention to the possible corruption of an art which ministers solely to pleasure, even to æsthetic pleasure? As it is, your 'pure' music has become corrupt, being vitiated by the material convention of Love. Where your music has remained pure is where it has remained decorative, where the art has remained accessory and not become independent. And decorative in this way music has remained as accompaniment to the religious services of the Catholic Church for instance, and in general, where it is an accompaniment to the occasions of life. Yes music is primarily an *accompanying* art—accompanying the singer in his song, the worshipper in his praise, the soldier on his march, the athlete at his exercises, and even the galley-slave at his oar. Music is truly the type of the arts, which should all be primarily decorative and so many accompaniments to life."

" Religious music, it is true, has remained accessory, or, as you say, decorative, but then Church music is dead music. It remains stationary, a good instance of hieratic, conventional art. And if decorative music is to be considered the type of all decorative art, then decorative art is indeed dead art. Expressive music, on the other hand, like all expressive art, is living art. Let us return however to the ' material convention of Love ' as you call it. You have not shown that it is a false convention, or indeed that it is a convention at all. If our expressive music has an erotic tinge, it means simply that our music gives expression to a fundamental human instinct, and far from being corrupted, as you maintain, by the emotion of Love, music idealizes the emotion, which itself is not false, but essentially real, having its basis in human nature."

" The emotion of Love ? Love is a sensation which your civilization has turned into a sentiment. The sensation is real, having, as you say, its basis in human nature. It is real enough to be used in Eastern art as a symbol. But what of the sentiment? Surely it is a fiction, and essentially false—a material convention. The sentiment of Love is unknown in the East, and as Orientals constitute a fair proportion of mankind, it is reasonable to conclude that Love as a sentiment is not rooted in human nature. And it is this sentiment that is a convention in your art and an obsession in your life. You talk of the Eternal Feminine, but with you the Feminine is Eternal and Omnipresent. You are not pantheists indeed, but you are pangynists, because you see Woman everywhere. You cannot regard nature

25

except with the eyes of Love, nor interpret life except in terms of sex. Where you might see the Divine, you see only the Feminine. Hence, I suppose that peculiarly Western phrase, 'a passionate love of nature'—a phrase unheard in the East. An Oriental sees God in nature, and so he tries to understand nature. Remember that our first duty to God is to know Him, the second to love Him, and that the greatest saints of the East and of the West passed their lives 'in meditation on the divine attributes.' One proof of the Oriental's sanity of vision in regard to nature is that he is never guilty of the 'pathetic fallacy' in his relations with nature. Nature he views as something comprehensible, and understanding it he uses natural forms as symbols and artistic patterns. A Japanese writer has remarked that a work of art is an essay on nature. The conventional designs of Eastern art are not artificial, being, in the first instance, drawn from nature. These conventional patterns really prove that the Oriental is familiar with all nature's moods and aspects. An Eastern temple is a revelation of man's consciousness of the forces of nature. The Egyptians raised monuments in the likeness of mountains—*instar montium eductæ pyramides*, as Tacitus observes. 'We feel in Indian temples,' says Lamennais, 'an infinite power of increase.' The architecture of the East conveys a sense of the mystery and the vastness of nature. In the decoration of their temples the artists betray their sensitiveness to all natural phenomena. They understand these phenomena and use them as symbols. You, however, view nature with 'romantic longing,' a diffuse desire, and where the Oriental grasps the comprehensible, you are overcome by the ineffable. And when you are thus overcome, you will not remain wisely mute, but forsooth must take to expression.

Could you expect romantic poetry to be other than incoherent ? *Je n'en vois pas le necessité.* The self-conscious expressions of romantic poets are gratuitous lies."

"But why lies ? Surely these poets express only what they feel."

"Yes—poor things ! But their feeling is false. Their passion for nature is born of the obsession of Love. And so their expression is false from the point of view of art. To a pathologist their expression may be true. It is certain to be interesting."

"I am afraid I don't follow you. You admit that the feeling of these poets may be real. Then, if they are sincere, their expression of it must be true. The feeling exists, they produce a copy of it. The line of art is parallel to the line of life. Truth in art consists in the parallelism of the lines."

"And parallel lines do not meet, being produced ever so far in either direction. But we Orientals believe that life and art are one. We say that in the beginning they were wedded, and it is our aim never to part them asunder. You—somewhat unnaturally— would start the universe on its course with a *decree nisi* for a blessing. And incidentally, let me remind you that as a metaphysical position the correspondence-theory of truth is untenable."

" How then do you regard truth ? "

" It is more reasonable to regard truth as coherence. 'Beauty is Truth, Truth Beauty,' because truth is coherence, and beauty is coherence,—and the test of coherence is stability. True art is a logical conclusion, with life for the major, and religion for the minor premise. Your art is dissociated from life, as it is divorced from religion. A disconnected art is a false art. Literally, it is an absurdity. Art for art's sake, expression for expression's sake, are contradictions in terms or tautologies. Your art in fact is, as you suggested, a would-be parallel line, for ever severed from life, or it is a vicious circle."

"But let us leave our poets and turn to our dramatists and novelists. You cannot, at any rate, say that they would be interesting merely as subjects for pathological study—since their art is not expressive purely for expression's sake. They aim at the portrayal of action and character."

"Ah!—portrayal again—still the fallacy of the parallel line. But after that preliminary criticism let us proceed. I said that the self-conscious expressions of your romantic poets are gratuitous lies. Your dramatists and novelists lie with a purpose—the most distressing form of falsehood. Your drama and your novel are didactic. They both contain some moral and expound some thesis. Even ' *Dorian Gray* ' is said to contain a moral. At least a section of the British public thinks it necessary to urge this point in extenuation of the book. Then, if even your romantic realists are moralists, are we to suppose that life itself contains a moral?"

" Why not?"

"If life contains a moral, it appears, as in your novels, at the end of the last chapter. For the moral of life is the fact of death. In form, at any rate, your dramatists and novelists are coherent. In this respect at least they are true to life. But the promise is deceptive. Both your drama and your novel are vitiated by false conventions of matter."

"How do you mean? Is their moral false? Surely not. And if their moral is true, they could not arrive at it from false premises. I will concede that the moral may be conventional since truth is always conventional."

"Ah, there you have exactly hit on the fallacy of your drama and your novel. Truth is not conventional, but your dramatists and novelists treat it as if it were. I mean that they present conventions for truth. And so the conventions become false conventions of matter— false, because unconfessed as conventions. You say, for instance, that your drama portrays character and action, and you believe that character creates action. This single notion of portrayal is sufficient to vitiate your drama. One could never produce a true, that is to say, a complete portrait whether of character or of action. You have deserted formal conventions in the drama for greater freedom to be faithful as you supposed, forgetting that complete fidelity is utterly beyond our reach. Wisdom is to accept our limitations; to recognize, first that conventions are necessary in art; secondly, and this is important, that convention belongs to form alone. In this way only can we attain such truth as is permitted us."

" Formal conventions in the drama! I must confess your idea strikes me as rather fantastic."

" I assure you I am quite reasonable. Consider the drama of the Greeks. In the Greek drama, as in the Oriental, the action is conventionalised, not the characters. You will remember Aristotle's insistence on unity of plot, and the minute details with regard to ' Recognition,' ' Reversal of Intention,' etc., laid down in the Poetics. The form of the play, that is the plot, was in

Greek drama frankly a convention. In your modern Western drama, on the other hand, you conventionalize your characters, but you do not admit the fact. You have your conventional types, and any character which departs from these you call 'unconvincing,' as though your conventional characters were convincing. But men cannot be forced into types. The types you create must necessarily be false—false through *suppressio veri*, and these lies are unconfessed. You say your art is human, but here you do violence to humanity in forcing men into categories. You hinder the spontaneous expression of individuality, and you ignore caprice,— unless of course you create the capricious character. You invert the natural order of things, and make the characters create the action, instead of letting the action reveal the characters. Given such and such characters, you are quite certain what will happen, although the only thing you can be certain of is that, given such and such characters, anything may happen. Your dramatists would make excellent private detectives for the six-penny magazines. Your characters, in short, are false material conventions. If you wish to inculcate moral lessons, why not frankly return to the Morality Play? That at least had no falsehood in it. The characters were acknowledged to be symbols. You are afraid to admit that your characters, your moral or immoral types, are merely cautionary signs, for fear of spoiling the moral effect of your plays. Consequently your signs are taken for entities, your puppets are taken for men. You do wrong to humanity in this—that in return men are taken for puppets by themselves. Numbers of young men and women in this city, I am told, journey nightly from the suburbs to the West-End by Tube, hoping to meet, not their affinities, but their 'types' on the stage; and having met and hailed their types, they are of course true to them ever after. It is terrible to think how many suburban *Ann Whitfields* have resolutely tracked innocent men to their doom since '*Man and Superman*' appeared. Yes, the inhumanity of western drama began with 'Euripides the human.' Greek drama before Euripides was ruled by the Oriental idea of Fate. If the Greeks exalted humanity in their sculpture, in their drama they depicted human impotence. Yes, the drama of the Greeks was an Oriental product, in spirit and in form. The plot in their drama was a convention symbolizing the unknown god, Fate,—and the canons of this convention were as rigid as are the canons laid down for the sculpture of a Buddha image in the East. The plot, that is to say, the idea of Fate, can be conventionalized without violence, but

individuals cannot be so conventionalized.
As it is you confuse human individuality
with dramatic personality, forgetting
that in the drama a *person* is the wearer
of a mask, the bearer of a rôle. You
imagine that your persons are individuals;
and here is the beginning of falsehood
and error. You present one aspect, a
fraction of an individual, and instead
of admitting that this fraction is in
truth a dramatic fiction, you maintain
that it is a real individual. But the
essence of an individual is that he is
indivisible, and must for ever remain
whole. There is an essential integrity
about a human character, which renders
any fractional representation of it
inevitably false. Of course, the fiction
that a dramatic person is a complete
character is necessary to your drama,
where you make the characters create
the action. You could not persuade the
most sympathetic audience that half-
characters could create action—that

rugged lie the public would refuse to swallow—so to make your fiction plausible, you persuade the public that your half-characters are whole characters, and the lie, thus smoothed and rounded off, is apparently quite acceptable. What your public ignores, however, is that the progress of your action, depending, as it does, on your characters, must necessarily be halting because your characters are maimed. Your action, in fact, is lopsided, it has literally an ethical twist, and like a centipede with some of its members amputated unsymmetrically, it crawls for ever in a vicious circle. Some of your more perspicacious dramatists, indeed, have realised this fact. Like all your artists they are self-conscious in their expression, and they are conscious, too, that their expression expresses nothing, that their 'action' takes nobody anywhither. So with that delicious naïveté which alone, if present, justifies self-consciousness, they call their plays *problem plays*. Some of your novelists, too, with an ingenuous lisp, call their novels *problem novels*, and your art critics, convinced that the problem is the last word in art, go to the Academy and look for problems in pictures. I am convinced that the romantic youth of the next generation will go to the Lakes, and look for problems under stones and riddles in running brooks. Yes, and when your dramatists do not embarrass you with their problems, they harass you with their propaganda. While half of them are framing riddles the other half solves them — garrulous sphinxes and indiscreet oracles. But why have you let pamphleteering die out as a vocation? In a by-gone age M. Brieux and Mr. Galsworthy might have found their calling. Dickens, with all his humour, mistook the function of the novelist when he used the novel to reform prison laws. Remember that when Milton wished to

treat of the freedom of the Press, he
wisely wrote a pamphlet instead of a
pastoral poem. Your modern dramatists
are capable of writing five-act tragedies
in blank verse to abolish the censorship
of the stage. Although Aristotle says
that in a tragedy the characters must
be persons in high estate, even so, I
refuse to believe that with such a theme
the Lord Chamberlain would make a
successful protagonist. No, your dramatists have no sense of the fitness of
things. Like your politicians, they
would not hesitate even to 'drag the
Crown' into the most paltry discussion.
You are clamouring for a National
Theatre. If you had it I am certain
you would abuse it, for you would use
it to discuss national institutions in. Mr.
Shaw would no doubt produce a 'play'
called ' *The Drama—a speech*,' wherein
he would explain that the House of
Commons should be disestablished, and
that dramatists should be paid £400 a

year by the State since playwrights really do the work of Parliamentarians. Meanwhile, what will become of the drama as a form of art?"

"Do you think then that it detracts from the dignity of an art to be used as an instrument of social reform?"

"Come, come, I appeal to your sense of decorum. Would not a proper Greek have been shocked if Zeus deserted the majesty of his throne on Olympus, usurped the function of the lame god Hephaestus, and set about tinkering? Would you turn your Muses into maid-servants?"

"Yet, a moment ago, you said that art for art's sake is a tautology, or a contradiction in terms, and now you complain that we make the art of the drama serve a useful purpose."

"A shrewd American observer once

remarked that the English have no idea
of good and evil, unless it be of a moral
good and evil. Similarly you seem to
have no idea of utility save of a purely
utilitarian utility. But there are kinds
of utility. The fact was brought home
to me by a remark of a young friend of
mine at Oxford the other day. He was
dining with me at a restaurant, and glan-
cing over the menu, he suddenly
exclaimed, 'That's useful.' On enquiry
I learnt that the thing he thus designated
as useful was a *pêche Melba*. The
designation was curious, but after all, it
was fundamentally reasonable. The *pêche
Melba* was useless from the utilitarian
point of view of nourishment. Still it
was quite useful, I might say it was
organic, in the whole design of the
dinner my friend had in mind."

"Your friend is a young epicure
then?"

"He appeared so to me, but he

apologised for the fact by explaining that a school of cookery had recently been established at Oxford,—that he was a critic of cookery, and therefore an artist in it, for the critic, he said, is artist."

"Did you know that your friend was plagiarizing Oscar Wilde?"

"I did, and I drew his attention to the circumstance.   But he excused himself by saying that Wilde held that there was no such thing as plagiarism, and that to prove it Wilde plagiarized himself as often as possible."

"An interesting young man !   In my time the young men at Oxford did not claim to be artists in cookery on the ground that they were critics of it."

"Oh no,—'Inasmuch as ye are critics, ye are artists,' is the cry after Walter

Pater. Before that they said with Matthew Arnold, 'Inasmuch as ye are artists, ye are moralists.' But to return to our *pêche Melba.* As that was useful inasmuch as it had its place in the scheme of my friend's dinner, so art is useful when it has its place in the scheme of life. But, as I remarked before, art for art's sake has no place in any scheme. Art for morality's sake, though less absurd, is still a perversion. You seem to ignore that there is a middle way between these two improprieties."

" And what is that ? "

" Briefly, art for decoration's sake otherwise art for life's sake. Art holds the same place in human life as the eye-brows do in the human face. The eye-brow is decorative. It is there not for its own sake, but for the sake of the face, and it is there because nature wills it so. You self-concious artists are

44

assiduously trying to cultivate eye-brows in space. True art, like the eye-brow is a spontaneous growth. Yes, art is a natural excrescence of life which we Orientals passively accept, but you are so sophisticated that you would have your lilies and roses toil and spin, hoping that thereby they will add to their beauty."

"You are severe. I suppose the creed of art for art's sake is somewhat of an exaggeration, but there is reason in the position. I admit the charge of sophistication that you urge against us. After all, knowledge to us is the greatest good, and if we act in a certain way, we act in the light of what we know. Let us say then, first that we realize that art is concerned with beauty. The excellence of art in general then is beauty, and there are several arts each with its own excellence. We believe then that art will realize its own excellence independently and in isolation, and the several arts their own excellences likewise. Our artists, each in his own province, study the properties and conditions of their arts, and so they produce works characteristically excellent in their kind. Our sciences too we regard in this way. We consider each science as an end in itself, and we have specialists in the several sciences. You cannot deny that in physics, physiology, psychology, progress has been made since each of these sciences was isolated, studied separately, regarded as an end in itself. So with art, we believe that art will realize its end, beauty, in fullest completion when pursued independently, for its own sake."

" And all this comes of sophistication ! Strange that you have not yet realised that knowledge is an evil, though your Bible tells you that the fruit of the forbidden tree was the fruit of the tree of knowledge. Knowledge is man's primal curse, when sought, as it was sought by Eve, for its own sake—from curiosity that is to say. Well, science cultivated for its own sake has, among other things, inflicted the curse of machinery on you, and art followed for its own sake has removed the blessing of beauty from your lives. You say that each of your arts, followed in isolation, has attained its perfection,—but tell me, if I wished to see the art of painting in London, where could I see it?"

" Oh, at the Academy, in the different galleries and collections, in several exhibitions."

" And if I wished to hear music?"

" There are several good concerts, at the Queen's Hall, for instance."

" Architecture?"

" There are buildings around you."

" Dancing ? "

" Well, if you wished to see good dancing, I suppose you would have to go to some of the music-halls, the Palace or the Coliseum. As you say, our ball-room dancing could hardly be called a form of art."

" But is there no graceful dancing in the country—in your villages ? "

" I am afraid not. Rustic dances on the village green belong to a by-gone age. Even the Irish jig and the Highland fling have come to the halls."

" There, I suppose, to attain their own excellence. And sculpture ? "

" In galleries again, and images of our heroes in public places,—and of course, in cemeteries."

" And if I wished to converse with

your wise men, your philosophers, where could I meet them ? "

" Our philosophers are to be found at our seats of learning, naturally, at our Universities, at Oxford and Cambridge for instance."

" You claimed a little while ago that expressive art is living art, but now you have proved conclusively that all your arts are dead arts. Has it never struck you that museums are the mausoleums of the arts? Your muses are apparently not virgins but widows, each emulating the Carian Artemisia. When art flourishes there are no museums. There were no museums in the East till you Westerners introduced them there, and still we don't understand them. What should we do with coffins when we have no dead? Picture galleries are the mortuary chapels of painting. In Mediæval Europe there were no picture galleries ; we have none in the East to-day. In the Middle Age in Europe painting was a decorative art, and as a matter of fact the art of painting in Europe attained its highest excellence some centuries ago, before you had evolved your theory of expression. Then the arts were content to flourish side by side, and religion wedded them to life, for artists created not to give expression to their personal emotions, but *ad majorem Dei gloriam,* and their works reflect their spirit. Western art has been most successful when it was meant to be purely decorative. You will remember Michael Angelo's decoration of the ceiling of the Sistine Chapel, and the frescoes by Ghirlandajo decorating the walls of Santa Maria Novella in Florence. Now your artists self-consciously paint pictures for the Academy. I went to the Academy a few days ago, and I couldn't decide which were the more self-conscious, the pictures or the visitors—both seemed to be intensely aware that people were looking at them. Here, then, is an art, splendid in isolation, complacently contemplating its own perfection. Believe me, when I first heard your Western phrase, 'the worship of Beauty,' I thought at first it was only a manner of speaking. I see now that you take your worship very seriously. *Mais, Messieurs, vous vous donnez en spectacle.*

And to hear music or singing, you tell me, I must go to a concert. Has it never occurred to you that music and song at these self-conscious concerts are as out of place as painting in a gallery? Music and song are not living, but dead and curiosities, when they are thus interred in concert rooms. A Mass sung at one of these concerts is as pathetic as a religious painting removed from its proper setting in a church and pinned to the wall of a museum. Do you kill your butterflies too on purpose that they may attain their excellence in a glass case? I remember you told me that religious music, which is a decorative art, is dead music. Which is more quick, the music that in church assists the worshipper in his praise, the music that rouses and uplifts all alike, or this concert-room music of yours, that is heard only by a few and affects only an infinitesimal part of the people? Religious music, you said, is dead music, a good instance of hieratic, conventional art. You must recast your notions of what is life and what is death in art. The conception of evolution is an obsession with modern Europeans to such an extent that you think that all change means life, and what does not move, or, as you say, progress, is dead. You confound life and mechanism, and you forget too that there are processes of decay. An art may be stationary for centuries, and remain vital in its effects, and the life of an art is seen in its effects. But you look to the product alone, and not to the effect, and so at your concerts and your art-exhibitions you show your still-born artistic progeny.

When I asked you where I might see your architecture, you said, ' There are buildings around you.' There are buildings and buildings. There are tin tabernacles, and there are cathedrals. Demosthenes referred to the public buildings as one of the chief glories of Athens. The Middle Age in Europe was an era of magnificence in architecture. But nowadays you build no beautiful buildings. You divide your arts into the fine or expressive, and the useful or applied. In the East all our arts are useful and decorative, so that when we make a building, we make it beautiful. ' All art is useless,' says Oscar Wilde, in the preface to ' *Dorian Gray.*' We say on the contrary, ' All art is useful.' Yes, even poetry and music are useful arts. You are too conscious of the distinction between *requisite* and *exquisite*. We try to make the requisite things also the exquisite things of life."

"That sounds idyllic—almost preciously so."

"It is true none the less, for in the East we live our idylls. As an instance of the preciousness of our common things, I might cite our every-day language. An English adventurer, Knox, writing of Ceylon in the seventeenth century, says:—'In this country the ploughman speaks as elegantly as the courtier.' You can divine the artistic temper of a people whose useful language is fine. It had not occurred to us to reserve the art of graceful diction for vellum-bound bibelots—therein to attain its proper excellence ; though, I suppose, the idea of a perspiring ploughman chanting the verses of a precious poet while he drives his team of oxen would not strike an Occidental in other than a humorous light. But, believe me, there is no element of humour in it, for the ploughman, though he thus chant his verse, is untouched by any aesthetic movement, and he speaks the language of the court singer because he knows no other.

You worshippers of beauty approach art too literally as a sacrament, and for fear of familiarity, I suppose, you do not approach it very frequently,—and when you do, you first self-consciously recollect yourselves into a mood of devotion. Your artists are your high priests. What does Horace say?

> ' Favete linguis. Carmina non prius
> Audita Musarum Sacerdos,
> Virginibus puerisque canto.'

Our artists are our ministers, and if our art is a sacrament at all, it is a viaticum not too good for our daily food.

The Greeks knew that art was made for man, and man was not made for art. They did not give the artist's calling the exaggerated dignity which you give it nowadays, for they considered the artist an artizan. Not that the Greeks had no reverence for art. And we Orientals, though we look on our artists as our ministers, revere art to this extent, that we strive ever to preserve it impersonal and universal. For the intimate is pollution in art, and vulgarity speaks always in the first person. An obscene work to us is one wherein the artist lays bare his soul, and many of your modern artists we should consider spiritual prostitutes. Art, you say, exists for its own sake, but you have gone a step further and made your artists ends in themselves. With you the artistic temperament covers a multitude of social sins. You would forgive your artists a crime against humanity, provided they gave you in return a *document humain.*

What wonder that your artists seek new and curious sins for art's sake? Art must progress—*n'est ce pas*—and life must keep pace with art. ' Life for art's sake,' cry your artists, and they surrender their lives to art. Our art is conventional; yes, and our artists are content to be *bons bourgeois*.

Accustomed then always to express themselves, I do not wonder that your artists are at a loss when they are called upon to produce a beautiful thing of use. The intensest personal emotion will not produce a beautiful public building. In architecture, the artist necessarily falls back on a more universal feeling; his inspiration inevitably comes from the consciousness of his people, and architecture more than any other art reflects a collective mood. Nowadays there is apparently no national sentiment among you vital enough to lend dignity and grace to the public buildings that you make. Religion is no longer a living force with you, so you build no great churches. The new Cathedral at Westminster is the only church conceived and built in Europe in recent times, in the spirit of the Middle Age, —but then the spirit of the Middle Age survives in Europe to-day only within the pale of the Catholic Church. Your art would be less paltry to-day, if religion were now, as it once was, a force in your lives."

" You remarked that art for morality's sake is a perversion. I don't understand how art for religion's sake could be less so. After all, religion and morality are the same thing."

" Religion and morality are absolutely distinct from each other. That this distinctness is a fact may be seen in the essential difference between an art inspired by religion and an art inspired by

morality. With you morality has taken
the place of religion, and your art has
suffered thereby. It seems to me that
you Northern Europeans have inter-
preted the Scripture text, 'Lay up
for yourselves treasures in Heaven'
rather too literally. You seem to have
a notion that Heaven is somewhere in
Lombard Street. You fancy that Heaven
is a huge banking concern. You start
an account there, you deposit to credit
whenever you perform a meritorious
action,—Kant has explained to you
precisely what kind of actions have
moral worth,—and when you commit
a sin, why—you issue a cheque on the
funds deposited. If that is Heaven,
the recording angel must be an expert
in the art of book-keeping by double
entry. We still believe, as you did
once on a time, that 'High Heaven
rejects the nicely-calculated lore of
less or more.' We do not calculate
the moral worth of our acts, but worship

God freely as our inclination leads us—'ex abundantia cordis os loquitur.' Your Kants and your Spinozas have produced metaphysical gods for you whom you worship with your intellects as you might worship the idea of the triangle. 'Art for art's sake—thought for thought's sake.' Knowledge is an end, and your thinkers self-consciously devote themselves to thought for its own sake. But self-conscious thinking defeats its purpose, and becomes mere psychological analysis. Introspection has produced your metaphysics and your various 'Absolutes' and 'Beings,' as still-born as your artistic creations. God is living when at the end of the day's labour the peasant makes the sign of the Cross and recites the Angelus, or when he turns his face to the west and worships the symbol of the sun. There is no God when the peasant is expected at eventide to meditate on 'an infinity of infinite attributes infinitely modified.' You have evolved a futurist art. I am afraid your modern religion too belongs exclusively to the future, for it certainly has no place in the life of the present. Your art is for the elect alone, and your religion is academic. Your thinkers have created their 'absolutes' in seclusion. Do you not imprison your wise men, your philosophers, in universities? The Magi of the East journeyed through many lands, following a strange star, until they discovered the Saviour, and worshipped him with offering of gold, and frankincense, and myrrh. Your modern Magi are busy with their intellects trying to explain, or to explain away, both the star and the Saviour."

"It is strange that you should depre- cate thought in this manner, seeing that in the East, in India, you had your caste of thinkers, the Brahmins. Surely that was carrying the principle of the speciali- zation of thought to its extremest limit."

"It was not thought for its own sake,

however, but thought for the sake of society. The fruit of this thought was seen in the social order of India, which was a partial realisation of Plato's ideal republic—the nearest approach to its realisation that has ever been made. The philosophers, the Brahmins, were supported by the auxiliaries, the Kshattriyas, and below these were the artizans, the Sudras. The philosophers in India were the law-givers and statesmen. In the East we interpret 'philosophy' literally as love of wisdom, and wisdom in the last analysis is practical. You often speak of the abstract thought of India, but our thinkers were our law-givers, and our knowledge was designed for use. Your philosophy, on the other hand, is in fact abstract speculation, utterly withdrawn from life."

"What of the contemplative ascetics of the East? You will not deny that they believe in contemplation for its own sake, just as our philosophers believe in disinterested speculation."

" That is a common Western fallacy. Eastern ascetics do not believe in contemplation for its own sake. They are convinced that life is an evil, and they hold that thought too, as one of the activities of life, is an evil. Their ideal is the negation of both physical and mental life. Such an attitude is rational, and is consistent. Aristotle says that happiness is complete activity. The Eastern ascetic holds that happiness is complete inactivity. Both views are reasonable, when we remember that they regard life from two different points of view. But whereas the latter view is complete reasonable, taken in itself, the former is intelligible only when we understand that activity means activity towards something, not activity for its own sake. Disinterested speculation is possible to the Deity alone, and your notion of thought

for its own sake is little short of
blasphemy. Men perceive only what
they are interested in, and when they
perceive they desire. The *theoretic* or
speculative life, the life of beholding, is
so called by analogy with the physical
function of sight. The intellect is the
eye of the soul. Now sight, as one of
your own psychologists has acutely
observed, 'is a prophetic function.'
Seeing, in other words, is not the
supreme but the initial act. We
instinctively go on to desire what we
perceive. A baby, for instance, almost
mechanically extends its hand to grasp
any object of whose presence it becomes
aware by sight. You may have observed
another curious phenomenon. Why does
a woman instinctively close her eyes
when she is kissed ? It is because, at a
certain point of attainment, the sense of
sight becomes incompatible with the
other senses. Sight, having fulfilled
its task of prophecy, becomes a positive

hindrance. The case is similar with the spiritual sight—the function of cognition. We contemplate, but contemplation is only a step towards desire. And this is the meaning of mysticism. Cognition is the prophecy, of which spiritual possession is the fulfilment."

"Well, you have shown that your thought is religious and mystical, while our thought is secular."

"And something else I hope—that your thought is academic, while our thought is popular. Yes, religious thought is always the profane thought, while secular thought is esoteric. But of course the fact that thought or art is popular is their sufficient condemnation in your eyes. You are all humanitarians, you are all eager to do good to humanity provided humanity does not assume equality with yourselves. You are philanthropists, *soit*, you love mankind, but for yourselves, you are supermen.

Consider the meaning of the word *Religion.* Does it not primarily mean a binding ? And when this bond unites a whole race together, does not the thought, the art, the living of that people become popular ? "

" Yes, religion is a bond, but if it unites a whole community, it separates that community from the rest of mankind. You said that an art inspired by religion is different from an art inspired by morality. You are right in this sense, that a moral art, being freed from the fetters of one particular religion, appeals to all mankind. A moral art is a human art."

" Humanism as an artistic creed has its place among the other cruelties of the Renaissance. It was born of the same spirit that produced the Borgias. Do you remember Pater's concluding essay in

his volume of studies on the Renaissance?
'Not the fruit of experience,' he says
there, 'but experience itself is the end.'
And again, 'Not to discriminate every
moment some passionate attitude in
those about us, and in the brilliancy of
their gifts some tragic dividing of forces
on their ways, is, on this short day of
frost and sun, to sleep before evening.'
Do you not see the essential inhumanity
of this point of view? Is not Humanism
the gospel of egoism? You say that an
art inspired by religion appeals only to
those who profess that religion, while a
moral art appeals to mankind. You do
not realize that your dream is impossible
of fulfilment, and fortunately so, for your
dream is a nightmare. Both Plato and
Aristotle wisely confined mankind within
the limits of a city-state, and when we
Orientals talk of humanity, we mean our
own community; for parochialism, not
cosmopolitanism, is the true creed.
There is one earth, but there are many

degrees of latitude and longitude. Different climates produce different breeds of men as they breed different kinds of plants. Art, I said, is a logical conclusion with life for the major, and religion for the minor premise. Art after all is a thing of use, and religion too is born of necessity. Men conceive their gods in conformity with the needs of their life, and needs vary with the climate. The different conceptions of the gods, always the sublimest conceptions of a race, are the different motives of artistic creation. So that you cannot produce a universal art till you produce a universal religion, and I doubt if you will produce a universal religion till you have produced one universal climate. You seem to think this last possible, for in anticipation of the achievement you are trying to persuade the human race to clothe itself in the European style. Art is an expression, yes—just as clothes are an expression. But what do rational clothes reveal ? The secrets, not of your soul, but of the weather. You will see the absurdity of an art that is to appeal to all mankind. The Parthenon expressed the climate of Attica and the worship of Pallas. The Taj Mahal expresses the climate of India and the creed of Islam. The Crystal Palace does not express Christianity ; nor does it express the peculiarities of the English climate ; for that reason it expresses the peculiarities of English taste."

" The Crystal Palace is not a church. It could not express Christianity in any case."

" I know—it is not a church, but a Palace of Art, a Temple of Beauty in fact. But art is meant to build temples, not to dwell in them. St. Stephen's is not a church, but as architecture, your Houses of Parliament do express Christianity none the less. Religion is the minor premise of art. Christianity gave you the conventions of the Gothic style in the art of building. Religion supplies the necessary motives for decoration. The end of art is first, use, then decoration. Expression is not a property, but an accident of art. You make expression the primary end of art, but the worst of such self-conscious expression is that it always expresses something beside what you mean to say. The Crystal Palace was meant to express your love of art. Well, it tells us of your love of art, but it tells us also that it was a misplaced affection."

" I suppose architecture as a medium of expression is sometimes unreliable. But that is because architecture is not primarily an expressive, but a useful art. Consider however some of our purely expressive arts,—music, poetry, or the art of the novel, which are free and un-hampered by considerations of utility.

Expression, I still maintain, is the end of art, and true art is purely expressive. Do these arts fail to fulfil their function? I spoke of an art which might appeal to all mankind. This art must certainly be dissociated from utility, for as you say, needs vary with the climate. Do you think the idea of a universal art, expressing in a free medium the common feelings of men, their vital emotions, to be really an impossible dream? I believe on the contrary that the dream has already been realized,—in the drama of Shakespeare, for instance. An art that mirrors mankind must appeal to men. Even our modern novels, which you decry, have their merits as portraits of human manners. I do not understand how any cultivated mind could fail to be fascinated by these narratives of the adventures of the soul. The analysis of the common emotions of mankind could not be without interest to a human being."

"There are no emotions common to mankind. What mankind has in common is a capacity for emotion. As for adventures of the soul, they are very well in their way, but most of your adventurers of the soul seem to end by discovering their own bodies. You do not appear to have observed, however, that the multiplication of these spiritual Odysseys must, of necessity, kill the possibility of spiritual adventure."

"Why so? Tales of adventure rouse curiosity, and stir the venturous spirit of their readers."

"Your tales of spiritual adventure do not whet curiosity, but satisfy it. I remarked that your modern drama and novel are didactic. They impart information, and they impart all the information that is available. Your human portraits are too realistic. Your art, as you say, is consciously expressive. Your psychological analysis of human emotion makes humanity incapable of emotion. Does not Yeats say that the West is emotionally bankrupt? You are incapable of emotion because you know all about it. Your dramatists and novelists, specialists in psychology, have made you too learned to be wise. And of course you cultivate knowledge for its own sake. Your novels faithfully delineate for you all the complexities of the emotion of Love for instance. Could you expect your young men and women to be ecstatic at springtide, when they know that a *grande passion* has its scheduled time as certain as a *grande vitesse*? Or could they, in sere autumn be subtilely linked in a soul-communion, in Maeterlinckian sweetness long drawn out,—when they know that Platonic friendships halt by the way? Who was it said that 'the nineteenth century dislike of realism is the rage of Caliban seeing his own face in a glass'? Caliban, when he sees his own face in a glass, proceeds forthwith to destroy the mirror. And Narcissus, when he sees his own image, destroys it by drowning himself in the mere. Your art, whose function is the conscious expression of emotion,

'Feeds its light's flame with self-substantial fuel,
  Making a famine where abundance lies.'

It is quite clear that self-conscious expression defeats its purpose, for it destroys the possibility of further expression, destroying as it does the possibility of further experience. And so you not only harm art, but mar life as well."

"Art is a *katharsis*—a purgation. By giving expression to our feeling in art, we cure our turbulent emotions, and so make our lives serene."

"It has been pointed out,—and indeed I believe it is now generally held—that by *katharsis* the Greeks meant not so much purgation as initiation, for the word *katharsis* was used by them in connection with initiation into certain religious mysteries. If art is to calm the turbulence of our emotions, it may do so only by initiating us into a mood of beauty, by inducing within us such a disposition that we may discern beauty where it is present, and reject what is not beautiful. Art is concerned with beauty, but so is life, and if serenity is a desirable quality in life, it is desirable in art as well. So that repression, not expression, is the secret of art, as it is the secret of life."

" Repression the secret of art ! Really you are too utterly fanciful."

" Is not the best life, as also the best art, selective ? You must not forget that scepticism is the better half of eclecticism. Repression means restraint, selection in expression, and it is only by following the principle of repression that we secure coherence and continuity of expression.

In the East we habitually repress our
emotions, and so we have not exhausted
our emotional capacity. For this reason
our art has been self-perpetuating. You
are emotionally bankrupt, because you
have always aimed at expression. You
have drawn too much on your emotions
for your art. You cultivate emotion for
the sake of its expression—and so your
art is self-destructive. 'Not the fruit of
experience, but experience itself is the
end,' says Pater. Does this mean
anything else than ' Emotion for the
sake of emotion'? But remember that
emotion is e-motion, a by-product.
The creed of Humanism has cruelly
mutilated mankind, for it has maimed
the emotional faculty of men. Ever
since the Renaissance the West has
misunderstood the meaning of art. It was
about that time that Europe became
self-conscious, and self-consciousness is
fatal to art, to thinking, to feeling, and
to living."

" On the contrary, by self-consciousness we double our living by making it
intense."

" Living should be not intense, but
intensive, for intense living kills life.
If you would truly be artists in life, do
not cherish, but chasten your emotions,
so that they become as rare as moods.
You are all æsthetes nowadays, but
become Philistines, like unto little
children, and you shall enter again the
kingdom of art. Living, after all, is the first
and best art, and if your modern art mars
living, you may be sure that it is false art.
You claim that your free and expressive
art faithfully mirrors mankind. On the
contrary, it is decorative and conventional
art that most truly reflects life."

" I see you are determined to be
startling."

" By your self-consciousness, you have
turned art from a mirror into a manual

of life, and a manual is generally a mosaic of hypocrisies. Yes, you make art serve the purpose of a diary, and you are too sophisticated to let the writing in it be naïve. Since the Renaissance, and its creed of Humanism, your art has been intimate and personal. You have always demanded novelty in art, and if art is to be perpetually original in this way, personality must also be bizarre. Ever since you became interested in man, using your art to ' paint man, man—whatever be the issue,'—ever since then, where your art has at all touched men, men have ceased to be genuine. Fortunately for them your masses are heedless about art, which is the luxury of the elect alone among you. M. Nordau has conclusively shown that for the last few hundred years, all your great artists have been degenerates—bizarre personalities, victims of the mania for novelty in art. One of your leading brain-specialists remarked the other day that he had dissected the brains of a lunatic and a post-impressionist, and he found that exactly the same cells were affected in either case. Your eccentrics seem to divine by instinct that art is their destiny. Their personalities are curious, their visions strange, and so you Humanists obtain your new types in humanity, your new ideals in art. Has it never occurred to you that it is inhuman to breed grotesque personalities for the sake of art? You worship beauty, and you sacrifice human victims on your altars. It is indeed fortunate that the masses in Europe care naught for art,— for, consider the probable result if the Irish peasantry regularly had seats in the Abbey Theatre in Dublin, and witnessed Mr. Synge's plays, or if the villagers of Wessex habitually read Mr. Hardy's novels of an evening. They would first become aware that they were picturesque, and then they would realize that picturesqueness is a quality expected of the peasantry by the cultured. The peasantry would in fact, with their sturdy common sense, turn to picturesqueness for a living. Self-consciously bizarre personalities among the elect are said to have the 'artistic temperament'; the same personalities among the peasantry would unhesitatingly, and with truth, be called criminals. Dartmoors would soon multiply in Wessex,—and should the Irish peasantry ever become interested in the art of the theatre, I am afraid the emergency exits from Ireland would be sought even more frequently than they are to-day. Such are the dangers of expression. Your art, however, has not always been so ethical and intimate and curious. Once on a time it was impersonal, in the Middle Ages, when you shared our secret of repression. The art of the East has always been anonymous and impersonal. Your art has been at its best when it touched life so closely that art itself was a mode of living, and personality had a representative aspect. In the East personality always retains a representative aspect, because the race-mood, the common thought of the race are clearly expressed in, and are so easily accessible through the convention. Yes, conventional decorative art is more truly expressive, and reflects life with better effect than does your expressive art. Your notion of expression is too one-sided, too subjective; for consider, the expressive quality of an object depends not on itself alone, but also on the receptive quality of the percipient. If language, for instance, is to be expressive, the speaker must be able to utter his thought in it, but the listener also must be able to understand it. Yours is a whimsical art, speaking always in some new esperanto. Your artists always speak of the public as barbarians, but it is your artists themselves that babble in strange tongues. They may be inspired, but life is not a perpetual Pentecost. You have a mystical conception of art as a Tower of Ivory, but it is only a Tower of Babel. A conventional art, on the other hand, is the common artistic language of a race. And that is why such art is always popular, for Beauty does not speak in a speech so fantastic that the pedantic only may take her utterance."

"Conventional art may be coherent, but it is also shallow. Conventions are a limitation, hindering free utterance, and if your art is always understood, it is only because it keeps saying the same thing."

"What matter if it speaks the truth? The test of coherence is stability, while the fickle is false."

"If truth is coherence, then the true is the varying, for coherence depends on conditions, and conditions change from age to age. The test of truth is not stability, but adaptability."

"But you love change for its own sake. You alter on speculation, and would make the moment fit your variation. Your art of the present is always meant for the future, and so it is a perpetual anachronism. You are reeds, but reeds that *would* be shaken by the wind out of consideration for a storm that may never come."

"You said that the expressiveness of a thing depends on the receptive quality of the percipient. Our art is difficult, because it is profound; but we are constantly trying to educate the public, to intensify the receptive quality of the percipients, so that art may not be meaningless to them,—instead of making our art so superficial that the ignorant may understand it. Our art embodies our ideals, and so it must always be in advance of the age. We look on art as an escape from life."

" It is corrupt to look on art as an escape from life. Only a corrupt civilization could breed such a perverted outlook. You say your art embodies your ideals. That remark explains much. You embody all your ideals in art, so that you can spare none for life. Hence, I suppose, the materialism of the West. Idealism for art, and materialism for life, —and art is distinct from life. Did you not say that you escape from life to art? —though few there be among you that essay the flight. In the East we keep ideals for life. You call us dreamers. But live some of your poetry instead of writing it, and spare some meed of beauty from your pictures for your lives. Yes, your art is always in advance of the age, for your artists are invariably telling this generation the secrets of the next. If an art is difficult of comprehension, it is unnatural ; and if it is prophetic, it is portentously so. If beauty has any message, it must be so legible that he who runs may read, for art is an incident of living, and beauty the accidental acquistion of use. Only the things that are needed for life are the objects of art, which is simply the further embellishment of these things for the sake of decoration."

II.

ON DECORATING ART.

.

II.

ON DECORATING ART.

"BUT what of artistic creation?"

"Decoration is creation, or at least the only sort of creation God has left us in this world, having anticipated, and perhaps exhausted the possibilities of the sort the West has been vainly reattempting these hundreds of years. Your notion of artistic creation is as blasphemous as your notion of the contemplative life. You are all Prometheuses, and this is your original sin. Creation in art is giving form to substance, and form is primarily dictated by utility. A vital work of art is one which has form. In art, design is the animating principle. 'Life belongs to form, not to matter.' You try to go a step further, and make substance, re-create matter. Consequently you make so many needless, apish things—a whole superfluous imitation of the original creation. You reproach heathens for making idols and worshipping them, but Western art is a worship of superfluously representative things—idolatry incarnate. You should not emulate God, not duplicate creation, but stay on earth and beautify. To beautify does not mean to make duplicates on a smaller scale— that is re-creating—but it means to decorate, to embellish. Art is really the decoration of art,—*ars decorare artem*— for art is concerned primarily with making the things that are necessary for life, and these useful things decoration beautifies. The artist is first artizan, then decorator. Perfect art is the perfect union of utility and embellishment. The end of art is to create delight in the daily exercise of our normal faculties,—briefly, to make a joy of life. Art is not an escape from life, but an alleviation of living, a *levamentum laboris*,—a recreation."

" I must confess that we hold beauty alone to be the end of the highest art. Considerations of utility must always interfere with the attainment of beauty, perpetually turning one aside from the true goal of art."

" I suppose you would be surprised if I tell you that, holding use to be the first end of art, we find beauty more often than you do,—if indeed, in your conscious search for it, you do not miss it altogether, for beauty, like happiness, is not found by those who seek it. In your conscious search for beauty, you ignore one of the first elements of beauty,—form, that is to say. Believing as you do that art is a re-creation rather than a recreation, you have been so absorbed in the re-creating of substance, in the vain attempt to make matter, that you have in the meantime completely forgotten the artistic value of form. "

" This is the most unkindest cut of all. I still hope your criticism is unmerited."

" I am afraid it is a true criticism. The conception of form is in the first instance derived from the conception of utility,—for form is the embodiment of purpose. In other words, it is nothing but the adjustment of means to ends. What are the ideas of *balance, proportion, symmetry, rhythm,* but refinements on this elementary idea of purpose? The human form is the visible embodiment of the function of man; it is in fact an explicit statement of man's place in the universe, and the shape of our limbs a definition of their functions as organs of the human body. Form then is meaningless apart from utility. Form is definition to a certain end. Beauty is our sense of beauty, our feeling of fitness. It is our perception of the nice adjustment of means to ends in things around us,—not a positive recognition of utility as such, but an awareness of harmony. Now in art you ignore this fundamental idea of utility. You deny the ulterior end that art is useful for, saying that art is its own end. Expression is the end of expression. As you have misunderstood the idea of expression in art, so you have completely misunderstood the idea of form. You seek form through expression; we let form reveal purpose—art being meant for use. As we always retain a sense of the utility of art we always retain a sense of the value of form. It does not need much thought to perceive the vanity of trying to achieve form through expression."

"All our artists attain form through expression. An artist in a work of art gives expression to a particular emotion. That emotion creates its own appropriate form in expression. The successful work of art is that whose form adequately expresses the emotion."

" Yes, you *are* trying to create substance nowadays. You cultivate

93

emotion for the sake of its expression. 'Not the fruit of experience, but experience itself is the end.' You try consciously to create emotion, the matter of your art, and let that matter in turn make its form. Hence your formless works of art, and your meaningless expressions. You tend nowadays more and more to deny form. Consider the work of Walt Whitman—there is emotion creating its own form—and Browning, and Wordsworth. Consider again the 'Blue Flower' romanticism of Germany, which produced a generation of artistic monstrosities, which you were quite willing to accept — for does not each emotion create its own appropriate form? Goethe wrote of one of these monstrosities:—'The standpoint to which philosophy has reduced us makes this degree of tolerance obligatory. We have learned to value the ideal, even when it manifests itself in the strangest forms.' A strange form is a monstrosity, because form is essentially conventional. The most beautiful expression is that which adheres closely to the rigid form, and the acceptance of limitations alone conveys a sense of artistic power. Consider the sonnet—one of the most beautiful of poetic forms, a convention bequeathed to you by Mediæval Italy. How many of your modern poets can use the sonnet-form gracefully? The sonnet calls for repression; therefore with you sonnet-eering is a lost art. The whole of Amiel's *Journal Intime* might have been expressed in a single sonnet, and had Amiel written one sonnet in place of his formless diary, his life would probably have been happier. However, he, too, believed in expression for its own sake, for he lived for the sake of his diary. 'Life,' says one of your critics, 'is terribly deficient in form.' I can understand the remark. If you make expression the end of art and experience the end of life, and deprive both of any ulterior informing purpose, your life becomes as formless and as void of meaning as your art. Theory always follows practice. As your art had become severed from all idea of utility, you say now, 'Art is useless.' In a few hundred years you will be propounding the maxim, 'Art is formless.' The old-fashioned among you still retain a sneaking respect for form. Form is to you a meaningless superstition, which your most enlightened and advanced minds have rid themselves of. Consider the Futurist school of painting, which is an outspoken recantation of form. You have created your matter, but you are quite content to leave it in a chaotic state."

" It is hardly fair to judge our art by the extravagances of the Futurist school."

" I am only following Aristotle's principle that the true nature of an organism is seen in its tendency or potentiality, rather than in its actuality. Pre-Raphaelitism was once an extravagance, but it reached the provinces, and became merely a vagary. With you the art of the immediate future is an extravagance; all the art of the past vagaries; while the art of the present is always the path that leads to salvation. No wonder you need so many museums and galleries to house your artistic waifs and strays. There is only one true way in art—the chaste and narrow way of convention; religion is its strait gate."

" I am afraid you are inclined to lay undue stress on the relation between religion and art."

" A conventional art is unintelligible without religion—for the alphabet of art is learnt in the school of religion."

" Such an alphabet must necessarily be rather hieroglyphical in character. Consider the hieratic art of Egypt."

" Hieratic art is the only democratic art. It was no doubt partly for this reason that Plato in the *Laws*, expresses his admiration of the stationary and hieratic character of Egyptian art. The art of Egypt was understood by the people of Egypt, whereas your art is understood by few beside the artists. The elect among you wear the orchids of art. To the mass of the natives of England, art is as meaningless, as little coveted by them, as is the orchid, for both are equally exotic. Consider again the art of Greece, also a conventional art inspired by religion. For this reason, and because it never lost sight of the idea of utility, the best Greek art was always popular. It was only late Greek that was consciously expressive. Alexandria was Athens become self-conscious. Theocritus only sings of the drinking-cup—'a deep bowl of ivy-wood, rubbed with sweet bee's wax, a two-eared bowl newly-wrought, smacking

still of the knife of the graver. Round
its upper edges goes the ivy winding, ivy
besprent with golden flowers; and about
it is a tendril twisted that joys in its
saffron fruit . . . .' Such bowls were
sung at self-conscious Alexandria, but
they were made and used in naïve
Hellas. While Longinus at Alexandria
analysed the sublime, Thyrsis attained
it in Sicily. Yes, Alexandria set the
modern fashions of the self-centred
university, of the museum, the picture
gallery, and the concert room. At
Alexandria man first became offensively
personal. But let us return to Athens
where philosophers discoursed in
Academe, among the plane-trees, still
happily unconscious that Academe was
an academy. Here art was impersonal.
Artists did not 'create' to express
themselves, but produced the things
necessary for the observances of religion
and the needs of daily life. Becoming
familiar in the service of religion with

the sublimest conceptions of their race, they used these conceptions as motives for the decoration of the useful things of life. The first conventions of the arts were learnt in the service of religion. Remember that the Greek drama was, from first to last, only the decoration of a religious festival ; that the theatre of the Greeks was vested with the same privileges of sanctuary as their temples ; that their dramatists and actors were, for the time being, priests with the privileges of the priesthood, the master of the ceremonies at this religious ceremonial being the priest of Dionysos. Was not the drama of the Greeks then a hieratic art, and popular for that very reason ? The Greek drama was essentially a conventional art, and its conventions—the limitation of the number of actors to three, the significant conventions of the mask and the buskin, and of the chorus, for example, were in the first instance prescribed by the priesthood. The idea of form, the principles of unity and balance which characterized all the art of the Greeks, were in the first instance derived from the drama, whose form was dictated purely by utility, the drama being consecrated to the service of religion. The form of the drama was embodied and exemplified again in their architecture, their sculpture, in their mural decoration and in their vase-painting. Is not the alphabet of art learnt in the school of religion? And whence did the Greeks derive the motives for the decoration of the things of daily use if not from religion? Herodotus tells us of numerous bowls and tripods, gifts to shrines and oracles. The decoration of these depicted scenes from their mythology, and the same motives were repeated in the embellishment of their vases, the ordinary vessels found in every household. The symbols, the conventional patterns of the decorative art of

the East are in the same way derived
from religion. We read in the *Ramayana*
that the craftsmen who wrought the
utensils for a religious sacrifice were
given the same privileges as the
officiating priests, who here again origin-
ated the first conventions of the arts.
Yes, art is meaningless without conventions, and conventions are unintelligible
without religion, or some other national
sentiment equally universal. You say
the convention hinders free expression.
Rational expression, as I pointed out,
demands intelligence on the part of the
listener, as well as reason on the part of
the hearer. A common sentiment like
that of religion creates such an affinity
between artist and public that the former
may merely hint and suggest his meaning
and be understood. Nowadays your
artist needs many friendly 'critics' while
he is living, and many well-intentioned
biographers after he is dead, to explain
'The Man and his Message,' and still

the public is bewildered. In the East the man is ignored. The personal message is the evil communication that corrupts good manners in art. In the East we are so old-fashioned that we will not accept these incoherent telegrams of art, though we understand and accept the traditional symbol. You will remember the Greek epigram commemorating a wall-painting by Polygnotus. The art of painting at this time was limited as a medium of expression, it was what you would call 'crude'; and yet it was said of the Polyxena in this painting 'that the whole of the Trojan war could be read in her eyes.' The mythology of Homer was then a living tradition. The epigram vindicates the crude style in painting for all time so long as there is a crude faith; and Polygnotus was a crude painter not because he was post-Impressionist, but because he was post-Homeric. Now-adays you affect crudeness because it is convincing, and cultivate naïveté for its charm. But is not self-conscious naïveté an absurdity?

You have abandoned traditions in life, and conventions in art—and I believe you are yourselves conscious of your loss. Consider the recent attempts to revivify and utilize the conventions of those early days when art was wedded to life. The fruit of these vain attempts you see in pre-Raphaelitism and its feigned naïveté, in pseudo-Catholicism, in an irreligious religiosity, a decadent primitiveness, a designed impressionism, a representative or pictorial symbolism— which are all contradictions in terms. Too late you have recognised the value of conventions, and when you have completely lost the sense of form, you will realize also the artistic value of form. It would appear that some among you are already troubled by a consciousness that all is not well with art when it is divorced from utility, and would wed them anew.

Only, as in your modern weddings, there seems to be some uncertainty as to which is to obey. Lately you have started ' Arts and Crafts Societies' and 'Schools of Design,' which only reveal your complete inability to make beautiful things of use. You are so perverted that you have succeeded in distorting that elementary idea of utility so that it is incomprehensible to the many, and made of that vital artistic creed merely a pretty artistic heresy. For centuries you had forgotten that decoration is the end of art. Now you present that early view of a decorative art in a form that is as self-contradictory as your other perversions."

" You credit us with a marvellous ingenuity in perversion."

" Your ingenuity has not been very subtle in this case, though characteristic. You have merely turned *decorative art,* into *artistic decoration.*"

" If the one is reasonable, I fail to see how the other is absurd. You are now juggling with terms."

" Think of the latest development in your art of painting—the School of Mural Decoration. Perhaps you have read the literature of the movement. I forget whether the movement has its official organ or not, and its head and branch offices, without which apparently no modern guild is complete. Anyhow this school has rediscovered decoration. Its members are willing to decorate any given blank wall—purely for love of the thing—and if the decoration is not successful, they are willing to efface it. Decoration, mark you, is the end— decoration for its own sake. As for walls—why, they are simply crying to be decorated. Here is a theory of utility for art's sake—a sufficiently comprehensive perversion. Unfortunately, the psychology of the movement is not original. The School of Pavement-Artists has for a number of years been tentatively decorating chance spaces of pavement, just as the School of Mural Decorators now proposes to decorate fortuitous expanses of wall. But why stop at mural decoration? A school of artistic wood-gravers might be started for the purpose of embellishing suitable wooden surfaces. You might send your useful chairs, tables, chests and other articles to be adorned in this way, and they would return completely beautified. So would all useful things be rendered beautiful by these artistic decorators. But the end of decorative art is to *make* beautiful things of use,—to make a beautiful building, decorate its walls if necessary, but first to make the building itself beautiful in form—not merely to decorate the walls of any formless building. Pseudo-craftsmanship is the latest development of your art, merely because in the Middle Ages the artist was the craftsman. Your modern mural decorator, because he is a modern artist, will merely turn the wall into a medium of expression. I have a friend, an artist and a mural decorator, who has succeeded in making his studio in Chelsea express what, I hope, is only a passing phase of his personality. He believes he is a martyr, a martyr to art, and to express his sense of martyrdom, he has made use of an eclectic and somewhat mystical style of mural decoration of one of the very early centuries A.D. His studio is in fact a most realistic reproduction of a catacomb—faithful to the last bird, beast, and little fish on the walls."

"Well his symbolism at any rate is appropriate."

"Yes the catacomb is a fairly successful symbol. The tradition of Christianity makes it intelligible as a symbol of persecution. My friend was wise in thus using a conventional symbolism, instead of trying to make his own symbolism to express persecution or any other idea, after the fashion of the Futurists. It seems to me that as a rule the West nowadays does not understand the true essence of the symbol, which lies in association rather than in representation. The connection of the symbol with the thing symbolized is a matter not of sight but of faith—not a matter of present imitation, but of old association. Hence all good symbols are conventions, and conventions are intelligible only in the light of living traditions. A convention is not a dead thing. The connection of a symbol with its object is not to be discovered in art, or manufactured artificially by art, but it is to be found and expressed in life, in actual living. Take for instance the symbolism of the Catholic Church, used to such good effect in your pre-Renaissance art. Had the form of life, the ideals of the Middle Ages remained stationary, these conventions would have lived longer, as similar conventions have lived in the East. But with the Renaissance the passion for personal expression sprang up, and swept away all traditions and conventions. Conventions are necessary in art. Nowadays each successive school of artists tries to create its own conventions, to make its own mannerisms conventional—a vain attempt. The absurdity of such efforts may be seen in that recent abortive symbolist movement in literature. Because the first symbols, those of language, were arbitrary, but only in the sense that we cannot now trace any inherent resemblance between them and their objects, past usage alone making present use possible, these modern symbolists fancy that all symbols are arbitrary. They try to make new symbols, but in characteristic fashion they set to work the wrong way, first choosing their symbols, supposedly on representative grounds, but the connections are so strained and capricious that the symbols are unintelligible. · Most of your modern art is therefore written in cipher, incomprehensible without an appended code, which you fail to supply none the less. Mr. Arthur Symons says, ' What distinguishes the symbolism of our day from the symbolism of the past is that it has now grown conscious of itself.' This self-consciousness is the first error in your modern symbolism. The moment you become self-conscious you go on to attempt the impossible task of re-creation. Whereas true symbols have grown spontaneously and unconsciously, you now try to manufacture them artificially, as a further aid to self-expression. Rimbaud's sonnet of the vowels does in a way tell the truth about all your modern symbolism :

'A noir, E blanc, I rouge, U vert, O bleu, voyelles
Je dirai quelque jour vos naissances latentes,
A, noir corset velu des mouches éclatantes
Qui bombillent autour des puanteurs cruelles,

Golfe d'ombre ; .   .   .   .   ' .   .   .

.   .   .   .

.   .   .   .

.   .   .   .

U, cycles, vibrements divins des mers virides,
Paix des pâtis semés d'animaux, paix des rides
Que l'alchimie imprime aux grands fronts studieux ;

.   .   .   .

Without some such key, the sound-mosaics of symbolist poets are as meaningless as are the colour-orchestrations of Futurist painters. The symbolist movement in literature is in fact the cult of language for its own sake, for you make language useless as a medium of expression, quite inexpressive, when, because words have significance you try to give significance to sounds, and because the composite word has meaning, to give meaning to the syllables which compose it. Language is the channel of thought, but too much meaning makes of language an incontinent river. Here symbolism, like futurism in painting, ignoring utility, is the complete negation of form. It is curious that ever since you made conscious expression the end of art, owing to this fundamental fallacy in your art-theory, your art in general defeats its purpose, and every new impulse in your art veers round to its opposite."

" In Eastern art apparently there are no new impulses of any kind. A useful, purely decorative art is the product of mankind in its infancy. Primitive peoples alone do not rise beyond a decorative art; and as for the symbolism of the Middle Ages, we have outgrown the ideals of the Middle Ages. Humanity has progressed since then."

" Humanity in Europe has simply grown aged. In the ancient East we still do not seek expression in art. Our art is still decorative and symbolical. It may be that repression is the secret of perpetual youth in the life and art of a people. Conventional symbolism keeps art for ever young. The realism of your art has left no place for symbolism."

" Greek art, before it attained its perfection, had abandoned the Oriental style of symbolism, which hinders the progress of art, forcing it into monotonous repetition, always giving to art moreover a monstrous and bizarre character contrary to reason. You still represent your gods crudely with six heads and a dozen arms. But the Greeks would not tolerate the grotesque—'to the Greek, pure artist, that work is most instinct with spiritual life which conforms most closely to the perfect facts of physical life.' The Pheidian Zeus was the Greek ideal, not some monstrous half-human divinity."

"You would make your gods in the likeness of men. God made man in His image and likeness, it is true, but you seem to think that God made only man.

Which is the more reasonable, the Oriental who refers back to the Creator all the attributes of all His creatures, man and beast alike, since that may not be in the creature which was not in the Creator, or the Greek who seeks to define the divine attributes into human form—and which embodies the more sublime conception, a monstrous or a humanly realistic image? Remember that at the present day it is uncertain whether many Greek statues represent gods or athletes. If the Greeks had been quite modern, and had the modern taste for financial economy in matters artistic, they would perhaps have made the same statues represent gods on the Sabbath, and football-players on Saturday afternoons. The Greeks derived their later conceptions of the gods from Homer. That these conceptions were not in any way sublime is sufficiently attested to by Plato, who realized that the gods as depicted by

Homer are only too human. That Plato would not tolerate poets and artists in his Republic is quite intelligible when we remember that he was familiar with the lusty divinities of Homer, and had seen the robust Apollos of the contemporary sculptors. That futile and truceless controversy among you between the artist and the moralist, first opened by Plato, need never have arisen if Greek art had always been as symbolical as at the first, without degenerating into realism. In the East, morality has no quarrel with art. The Oriental is the complete Platonist, and the principles of Plato's philosophy are reflected in Oriental art. Plato said that the painter's representations of objects are thrice removed from the truth. The Oriental would certainly agree with this criticism, for the Eastern artist never tries to reproduce the external forms of nature, but rather to represent the Ideas which they embody. Remember that to the Oriental, who believes in metempsychosis, the doctrine of reminiscence is something more than a picturesque allegory. The Eastern artist in fact goes back to the realm of original Ideas; before he makes an image he retires into solitude and meditation. The genius is, without metaphor, the seer of visions. In this way it was that the first images of the gods were made by Orientals—literally they were the embodiments of mystic visions. The image of the god once visualized is thereafter made conventional, the symbolism prescribed by canons. The wealth of symbolism in Oriental art was derived in this way as much as the symbolism of the Catholic Church is drawn from the visions of mystics—only the Catholic mystic was, as a rule, poet rather than sculptor or painter. Yes, the symbolism of art is always learnt from religion. I do not suggest that art is for ever to be the handmaid of religion—both religion and art are equally incidental and accessory to living—but to art religion stands in the place of a necessary, anterior circumstance. The religion of a people reveals that people's outlook on life. A religion is an attempt at interpreting the universe, and symbols suggest the connections we have discovered. Art is initially dedicated to the service of religion, and in return for this first service religion bestows on art the gift of symbols, which is the gift of tongues."

"A religion is one of the earliest attempts at interpreting the universe—symbolism a language adequate only to the expression of that first interpretation. Symbolism in time becomes a dead language, for with time we modify our earlier conceptions. Nothing is so mutable as truth."

"Our conceptions of life, that is to say, the necessities of our life vary. But as

a religion acquires new dogmas in
accordance with varying conceptions,
so art gradually acquires new symbols."

" But why should we leave art always
in bondage to religion ?   And why need
art always speak in symbols, instead of
expressing   the   truth   clearly   and
directly ? "

" Because nothing is so mutable as
truth.   Art expresses our apprehension
of truth, art is a manner of seeing.
Seeing after all is relative to its organ,
and as for the organ of sight, its
efficiency varies with the need of the
moment.   In short our vision is never
reliable. We never apprehend the truth.
The   symbol   by   its   very   inadequacy
reminds us always of the incompleteness,
of the subjectivity of our seeing.   It is
the symbol alone that saves us from the
convention of matter in art.   The Eastern
artist knows that the world is a fleeting

illusion. For that reason Eastern art is not a permanent delusion. Your art is always false, abounding as it does in material conventions."

" Then is a comprehensive scepticism the last secret of art ?"

" Scepticism is the intellectual privilege of the believer,—and a comprehensive scepticism may only proceed from an all-embracing faith. The order of the universe is the balance of opposites, and Providence is the rendering of compensations. If you would disbelieve in everything you must believe in everything. If you would doubt phenomena you must believe in Ideas. You may hold that the world is an illusion, but you must then hold that the world is a symbol. The materialist may not be a symbolist. Art may not be realistic and symbolical at the same time. There is a certain mediatory quality which is of the essence of the symbol. Western art may not use symbols because Western civilization has been a universal process of mistaking means for ends. I believe you give the process the name of specialization. Art is an end; thought is an end; education, emotion, experience, all these are ends; democracy itself which is nothing but a means is also an end with you. We can only use that as a symbol which we are sufficiently aloof from, sufficiently master of, to look upon it as a means. You cannot regard the world as a symbol because you are materialists. Your art is the expression of emotion. Hence you may not make a symbol of an emotion, but only represent it."

"Does that fact detract from the excellence of our art?"

"Yes, because art is impersonal. The representation of an emotion is always a personal representation. An impersonal art has a higher degree of excellence than a personal art for the same reason that made Aristotle say that poetry is a more universal and truer thing than history. Your art in fact is a series of petty, personal histories. The symbol, being a race-product, and adequate only to the expression of race-moods prevents the artist from personal expression which is fatal to art and also to life. The symbol which is an abstract convention makes art always preserve its universal character,—and so art reacts on life in this way, that we in turn become selfless and see in our lives only the working of universal laws. It is only in this way that we attain serenity in life. It is thus that art initiates us into a mood of beauty, and calms the turbulence of our emotions. Consider the conventional image of the Buddha. To the serenity expressed in that symbol is probably due the serenity of Eastern life. Symbolism in art has this further merit, that it offers the only solution to the feud between artist and moralist. Plato was quick to detect the fallacy of the theory that the representation of emotion cures emotion. Consider what he says in the Republic :—

'And with regard to sexual desires, and anger, and all feelings of desire and pain and pleasure which we say follow all our actions, you observe that poetic imitation produces all these effects in us. They should be withered, and it waters them and makes them grow. It makes them rule over us, when they ought to be subjects if we are to become better and happier, instead of worse and more miserable.' Your modern novel can hardly touch matters of sex without becoming realistically pornographic. In the East sex is used always only as a symbol. The Eastern moralist has never had occasion to protest against the corrupting influences of literature or art."

"I admit that there are still some Puritans among us who seek to limit our art, but happily Puritanism is no longer fashionable."

"Long centuries ago the English people had a genuine character of their own. Perhaps the Tudor period represents the English national temper at its best. But just then you were carried away by the Renaissance movement, and in reaction you let yourselves be bullied into Puritanism, and now you are letting yourselves be bullied out of Puritanism into pure vulgarity. Even a genuine Puritanical taste is preferable to an utter want of taste, and good broad-cloth is better than bad brocade. Between Puritanism and vulgarity you have lost sight of your national character and your traditions. You need mightily to be converted and ' find yourselves.' In the Tudor times when you were true to yourselves, your art was more nearly joined to life than it has ever been since. Your art then was decorative, and life had really the quality of a pageant. Taine remarks of life in Europe at the time : ' This is why at this period they did make a holiday of it, so like a picture that it fostered painting in Italy, so like a piece of acting that it produced the drama in England.' The drama in England does not mean Shakespeare, for Shakespeare really represents a departure from the genuine English tradition of the drama as a decorative art. With Shakespeare the English drama became consciously expressive. The earlier English drama was only an added decoration to life, the embellishment of an occasion. That earlier tradition we see represented in the exquisitely decorative *Midsummer Night's Dream*, for it was a masque, made for the adornment of some occasion in life. It was a beautiful thing meant for use. Such has the drama always remained in the East, a joyous thing meant only for decorating life and making life joyous. The self-conscious, introspective and moralising *Hamlet* is a typical Renaissance product. It is ethical, and 'human' and consciously expressive. It was written for the theatre, written by Shakespeare to express Shakespeare. When the *Globe* Theatre was built in London, English drama was in its decline, for it had become conscious of itself. And the quality of English life too began to deteriorate. You seek now to restore to life something of the quality of a masquerade, but you should not in the first place have let the theatre absorb the masque. Shakespeare had a supreme sense of irony when he said that the world is a stage after he had done his best to deprive life of its spectacular element. When the stage was removed from the world to the theatre, life was made the poorer—it lost the quality of a show. The specializing of art is the disintegrating of life."

"But has not art gained, and has not life shared in the gain? *Hamlet* is an acquisition to life as to art. As you say, only an expressive art could have created *Hamlet*, and in this case the artist seems to have succeeded very well without symbolism."

"Specialization is a loss to art itself. The acceptance of a theory of conscious expression is the beginning of art's quarrel with itself, for you soon come to the problem of the ugly in art. Your artist is given full licence to express himself; then if his feelings are painful or morbid, or if he sees only the ugly aspects of life, he is free to represent the morbid and the ugly in art. The representation of undesirable things in art gives these undesirable things a fresh tenure in life. Every young man is a

Hamlet nowadays as soon as he has attained years of discretion. The worm of introspection has definitely taken up its abode in life's rose-garden. Plato was distressed to think of ' the best of us listening to Homer or any other of the tragic poets, when he is imitating a hero in grief, and spinning out a long melancholy lamentation, or imitating men singing and disfiguring themselves in grief.' When we see these things done in art, we go and do likewise in life ; and these things are ugly in life. Here too you see the loss to art when you deserted symbolism. Representation renders selection in art unnecessary. The imitative instinct embraces everything. When you make the artist's craving for self-expression the basis of art, rather than the beautifying of life, you give ugliness a sanction in art, and evil a sanction in life. Conscious expression has no place in art. When decoration is the end of art, the artist's opportunities for self-expression are limited, and the ugly is rigorously excluded from the province of art. And so we gradually eliminate the ugly elements from life. Now, since your artists do represent the ugly in art, you are forced into the exaltation of ugliness. The ugly elements increase and multiply in life, and your art instead of making life beautiful, makes life hideous. In the East life remains beautiful because art is decorative. The morris dance, once, like the masque, common in England, belonged to the time when art in England was decorative. In the East we still have our decorative dances, we can still contrive a gorgeous pageant for a feast-day, and when we are joyous we crown our brows with garlands."

" Oh, the prettinesses of unsophisticated peoples ! "

" Do not sneer at unsophisticated prettiness. Unsophisticated prettiness comes very near the sublime—it is as near the sublime as we can ever attain to. The prettinesses of the East are the formal conventions of living. They do not proceed from a sophisticated cult of prettiness for its own sake. The decorative art of the East is so closely wedded to life that it makes life beautiful, it moulds life after its pattern. Decorative art inasmuch as it is useful, is necessary to all, and inasmuch as it is conventional it is understood by all. The formal conventions of art are repeated in the formal conventions of life, for their symbolism is identical. Consider the decorative dancing of the East. Here the fleeting gestures and attitudes are derived from the symbolical poses of the gods in the sculptor's art, and because dancing is graceful and dancing is common, rhythm and grace are not lacking in the motions and postures of daily life. The flowers in the garlands worn on festal occasions are chosen for the same symbolism which directs their choice in the decorative art of the carver in precious metals. The weaver in making his carpets uses as his patterns the geometrical symbols first designed by mystics, and used afterwards in decorating the walls of temples ; and the potter embellishes his vessels with the conventionalised forms of trees and animals as wrought on temple pillars. Common speech is the diction of prayer, and as the first prayers or spells were made by poets, the speech of daily life is not wanting in the quality of enchantment or at least of courtesy. Could art be more one with life than here where art has become the habitual manner of living ? The symbolism of art permeates life. Life, not art, is the sacrament ; and art, by use, becomes as it were a second nature. Here art is not specialized, but life is organized. The activities of religion and art are subordinate to that supreme activity which is living. Decorative art is true in this, that it does not mar, but moulds life. If the end of art is to produce beauty, the fruit of art is to be seen only in living, for beauty is attained not by understanding but by use; the conscious formulation of its principles does not produce beauty, but harmonious living illustrates its idea. If there is an idea or principle of beauty, our senses give us the first intimation of its existence, and decorative art aims at the wide diffusion of sensuous beauty. Plato insists in the Republic on the importance of a beautiful decorative art—the only art he would permit in the ideal state. The craftsmen in the ideal state must be skilled in the making of beautiful objects, so that the young, becoming familiar by the senses with the beauty of material things, may grow from their earliest years 'into likeness and friendship and harmony with the principle of beauty.' Yes, decorative art is our first education in beauty, and it is a compulsory education.

Art is made a part of living, and none may plead that he has not the leisure for it. Its end is to make a pleasure of toil—to make a delight of life. It embellishes those things which are made to meet the ordinary necessities of life, and gives pleasure to the senses which are the first instruments of toil. Decorative art is productive of beauty in this that it cultivates in all alike an instinctive intolerance of ugliness. It generates the beautiful living, which in its turn generates beautiful art, and so beauty is perpetuated. Love and art are both concerned with beauty, not with beauty alone, but with the generation and reproduction of beauty.

> 'From fairest creatures we demand increase,
> That thereby beauty's rose may never die.'

If beauty is the end of art, your art completely misses its end. The artist's need for self-expression is the basis of your art. Expression is fatal to the spirit of selection, so essential to the perpetuation of beauty. On your art-theory you cannot logically exclude the ugly from the province of art, and as most of your artists are obsessed with the ugly nowadays, you secure a perpetuation of ugliness."

" Art ceases to be true to life if it ignores the facts of life. If our art includes the ugly, it is because our art takes all life for its province. Art at least should be free from prejudice. "

" Beauty is a prejudice.   Art seeks to vindicate the ways of man to man. But this vindication is possible in two ways. One, which is the better, is to fashion our ways after our prejudice. This is the way of the East. The other, which is the worse, is to fashion our prejudice after our ways,—that is to uproot our prejudice, to destroy art. This is the way of the West."

Lightning Source UK Ltd.
Milton Keynes UK
UKHW031116230821
389329UK00010B/831